INTERVENTION

A Story of Grace

RICHARD SMITH

Intervention (A Story of Grace)

Author: Richard Smith

Cover design: "Book cover designed by JD&J with stock imagery provided by @123RF.com."

ISBN: 978-0-578-45159-6

TABLE OF CONTENTS

Introduction

You should write a book. That's what so many said after hearing stories about my life. However, without thinking twice, I'd dismiss the idea of writing a book every time I heard it. It wasn't until I realized just how frequently this statement was rolling out of people in conversations that I began to wonder if this idea was more than it appeared and that it was a command rather than a suggestion. I considered the fact that this may be my calling and something God wanted me to do. Yet, I did nothing with it.

I sat on that idea until one day God intervened in a unique way. It was at the end of a long day, as I was home spending time with my family, the phone rang. My wife picked up first, but within seconds, she turned around to get my attention. It was one of the senior mothers from the church I attended, and she was on the other end asking for me.

"Minister Smith," the senior mother asked with urgency in her voice, ensuring my wife had handed the phone over to me. "Yes mother, it's me," I replied. "Turn on the television, now, she said." "Okay, but." "Turn to channel 24," she interrupted. Before I could get another word out, she hung up. I could tell she wasn't playing around so I didn't attempt to call back to ask why. I did as I was told and hastily turned the TV to channel 24. To my surprise, there was a young man being interviewed about a book that he had written. He stated that God had led him to write the book and that when he was obedient and followed through with writing it, God used it to impact a lot of people. He was completely amazed at all that had happened in his life after writing his book, and there I was, completely amazed at everything he was saying. It sounded like the story of my life. I stayed glued to the TV until the guy finished talking about his journey. The moment it ended, I called the church mother back.

"How did you know?" I blurted out as soon as I heard her pick up. "Writing a book has been on my heart all day! That interview was exactly what I needed to hear. How did you know?" "I didn't know anything about you writing a book or what was on that channel," she laughed. "The Holy Ghost told me to tell you to turn your TV to that specific channel."

I was floored and blown away all at the same time. It was such a significant confirmation for me to do what was already in my heart. From that day on, I couldn't turn back. I started to make moves in that direction. Writing this book took a few years. While trying to complete it, I endured an unbelievable amount of turmoil and disappointment. I have had setbacks in my health, which unfortunately still impacts me, as I am in pain every day to some degree. I suffered severe financial difficulties. Then, I made a difficult transition to a new city, all while continuing to terribly suffer in both my body and finances. I also struggled with the feeling of pride in my heart when the stories of my life started to take shape while writing this book. I realized just how much I didn't want others to know about me. I wanted to draw back and give up and allow some of these stories to remain untold. However, through it all, I learned to relinquish my sinful pride so that this book could be completed and made available to the people who need to read it. I had to follow through with what God called me to do, even if that meant tearing down my defensive walls and fully opening up.

I believe one of the greatest things a Christian can do is be open about his or her failures and flaws. Why? Because in doing so, others who are struggling in the same areas can see a witness of God's power to love and restore even the most broken individuals. Essentially, this book tells the story of a broken individual who has received an abundance of grace and mercy throughout his lifetime. This book stands as a witness of God's intervention in my life. As you dive into my story, I pray that it ministers to your heart in an amazing way.

Prologue: Five Seconds to Run

EARLY IN LIFE, I learned how to enjoy being alone. I rarely had any friends to play with, so on many occasions I enjoyed evenings of fun by myself. My family and I lived in a compact, 10-unit apartment complex in the small town of Bearden, Arkansas where everyone knew each other. I frequently played alone in front of our unit and my parents had no reason to worry about my safety. There were very few dangers around town. At that time kids played outside well into the evening hours and nothing ever happened to them.

One evening, my playing ventured a little farther than usual. When I reached the edge of our building, I noticed a guy standing in the pathway. I recognized him. I didn't know much about him, besides the fact that he suffered from a mental illness and that he was somewhere between 18-19 years old. Still, he had always been nice and never a threat. Except, this time, something seemed a bit off. He looked at me intensely while cracking an odd smile, his right hand hidden in the pocket of the large trench coat he wore. I knew instantly that something was wrong. He revealed that he had a gun. "You have five seconds to run as far away as possible and then I will begin shooting." I froze in fear. Do I call for help? Do I scream? What do I do? "Run now" he yelled. He wanted to see if I could outrun the bullets of his gun. I didn't move; I knew that I could not run faster than bullets. I could tell that reasoning with him would be impossible. "Run!" He shouted angrily. My feet stayed glued to the concrete.

Suddenly without hesitation, I did something that neither he nor I expected. I answered back. "Go home," I yelled with as much fire as a child's voice could possibly create. I saw his mouth start to move, to utter some words, but I interrupted him. "Go home," I repeated. This time with more force. "Go home," I yelled again. He took a few steps back. I repeated it again, and he moved back further. Each time I spoke, he'd take more steps backwards. After telling him to go home more times than I could count, he was out of my sight. My heart continued to race from the adrenaline of the moment as I ran to my apartment unit.

When I got inside, I kept quiet. I didn't tell anyone what happened, ever. I have been silent about that day until now, as I write this book. As I reflect upon that moment, I see how that incident marked the beginning of many incidents to follow. There would be several times in my life when I would find myself in danger, but somehow, God always made a way for me to escape the danger or some form of temptation, which would have destroyed me.

There is no way that I would have spoken up to that guy in the way in which I did that day on my own. I truly believe God gave me the boldness in that moment. Months later, I heard about another incident he was involved in, and I learned more about his mental state. I then understood the danger that I was really in on the day that I encountered him. It could have been me. I could have been his victim.

(1)

Transition to El Dorado

I GREW UP in a Christian home. Going to church was second nature for us. My father was a minister and my mother was also very active in the church as well. From birth, I was taught Biblical principles. My parents not only taught me, and my siblings' biblical principles, but they also modeled them before us.

Watching my father, I was in awe of his strong connection with God and the gifts and abilities the Lord had given him. There were times when he would speak of something specific that was going to occur, and sure enough, it would happen just as he said it would. There were times when he warned me to stay away from certain individuals. I would comply and later see the meaning of his warnings due to something occurring in those individuals' lives that would have affected me if I had continued to spend time with them. I remember on one occasion, I was thinking some not-so-good thoughts and he told me exactly what I was thinking. From that moment on, I made sure my thoughts were pure when I was around him. There were critical times in the lives of my siblings and I while growing up, in which, we were in some form of danger or about to make a very bad decision, and my father would suddenly show up and prevent disaster. He would pray for us when we were sick, and we would feel better. I learned that God truly existed by watching my father. I knew that no human being could function the way my dad did without God.

At church, I enjoyed meeting other kids and listening to the testimonies of how God had done what seemed impossible in their lives. I also loved the praise and worship, but what always fascinated me was the preaching. Watching a minister preach God's Word had a tremendous impact on me. I especially loved listening to my father preach. My dad had a unique preaching style in comparison to most of the preachers I was accustomed to hearing. Our church was very charismatic, but he didn't display a lot of emotion in his sermons. Rather, he plainly presented the scriptures with commentary. The anointing that God had placed on him allowed his words to have a significant effect on me.

This was life in Bearden. Home, school, church and then repeat. All seemed well, and I had no desire for more than I already had. I felt like I had everything a kid could desire. The early years were a wonderful time, but the good times were about to significantly change. My family and I spent the first 6 years of my life in Bearden. After completing 1st grade, my father came to us and said the Lord was leading him to move us further south in Arkansas to a city called El Dorado. Bearden was a nice small town and many of my relatives lived there. In Bearden, I could walk alone to my grandmother's house as a little boy and my parents had no reason to worry about me. There were dangers, but nothing in comparison to the dangers I would encounter in El Dorado. The entire family was not happy about the move to El Dorado. We were overwhelmed with a heavy weight of sadness as we considered the transition. Looking back on the move, I can now see that it was God's will and His plan was awesome. I admire my father for doing what God led him to do even though it was extremely difficult, and his family did not support the decision. There will be times in each of our lives, when God will call us to do things that are impossible for us to do on our own so that we will have no choice but to rely on Him. Through our obedience despite the difficulties and hardships, we bring Him glory.

Life was completely different in El Dorado and unlike anything I had ever experienced. In this new environment, I was forced to engage in fights. I had never done such a thing before we moved to this city. I hated fighting; I would never engage in it unless there were absolutely no alternatives. Fighting was a very foreign and meaningless concept to me. On one instance, a friend in the neighborhood threw a basketball and hit me with the intention of hitting my sister instead, who was harassing him, so I chased him with a large, two-by-four piece of wood. The ball had hit me in front of several other guys in the neighborhood, so my pride led me to chase him, but I had absolutely no intentions of hitting him with it.

While walking home from school the following week, he met me while many others were around and punched me. Blood from my lip splattered on my new shirt that I was wearing for the first time. I chose not to hit him back. I had embarrassed him, and now, he had embarrassed me. We were even, but then everyone around me at the time started calling me soft, and a coward so I had no choice but to fight, because I was extremely angry at that point. I was about to make a major mistake, because I had picked up something sharp to stab him, but suddenly the mom of a neighborhood friend was driving by and stopped. She had him get into the car with her and she drove off. I was livid. This dude just embarrassed me and now he gets away. Looking back, I am so glad that God sent that lady to come and get him. The time between that day and the next time I saw him gave me a chance to let it go. He and I were good friends after that.

Fighting was a way of life in the neighborhood we lived in and at school also. During my first day at school in El Dorado, a fellow student decided he would beat up the new kid — me! I decided to let him know that it wasn't the right choice. After I punched him a few times, he quickly realized that he had made an unwise decision and began to ask other students for help, but none of them chose to assist him.

I could fight if I absolutely had to, but it just wasn't me. However, in this new environment, showing any form of weakness marked you as easy prey and there were plenty of predators around. The foundation of the problem was that the only thing that most of the youth considered themselves to have was their pride, and when that was taken, there would be drastic consequences. If a person lost a fight, it could escalate to something far greater than ever intended.

There were many moments of divine intervention by God to protect me in this unique environment. My brother and I were playing on a street corner one day and suddenly, an argument between two individuals only a few feet from us, escalated into a shooting and led to us running as fast as we could towards home. I will never forget the reaction of the person who was shot. The agony and pain was evident on the face of the individual who had been shot. The loud cry of the victim revealed that getting shot was no joke.

On another occasion, I was playing basketball in a local park, and after my team had won the last game played, a player on the other team pulled out his gun and began shooting upward. By shooting straight up into the air, he clearly only wanted to scare us while venting some frustration simultaneously. Shortly after this incident, the same guy shot and killed a friend of mine who frequently visited my home, during a dice game. The same anger he had during the dice game was likely the same anger he had after the basketball game that I played against him. It was by God's grace that I, and those on my team during the basketball game didn't become victims of his internal rage. One day, while playing in a local park, I saw a friend being beaten by a guy and I rushed over to help. I didn't touch the guy beating my friend. I simply told him to stop and he looked at me with complete hatred in his eyes. He stopped and gradually began to walk away. He was much bigger than we were and could have easily handled both of us if I had decided to attack him. We were just kids and he was in his late teens. What I didn't know at the time was that he was very dangerous. Later, the same guy would commit murder. He could have killed one of us that day, but God didn't allow it.

Despite this, the neighborhood and city itself was far from being the worst in America. There were plenty of good days filled with fun and there were many good and amazing people around me as well. When I encounter anyone from El Dorado, I always feel as though I am greeting a family member. I learned during this time that God was Jehovah-Nissi, (My banner of love and protection). I could mention more stories of protection, but these that I have mentioned are sufficient enough to convey the characteristic of God as protector.

This was life in El Dorado, chaotic at times, filled with hardship, yet possessing moments that I will cherish forever. It was a time that contained things that could lead you to tears, but also held moments, which brought extreme joy. I love that town and the people in it and from it.

(2)

Many Missing Men

MY SIBLINGS AND I spent most of our time with our stay-at-home mother. Along with a lengthy commute, my father worked very long hours at his job. There was a period that I would wake up in the morning and he had not made it home from work and I would go off to school. When I returned from school, my father had been home and returned to work again. I don't know how he was able to do this.

During this time, my friends thought that my mother was a single mom and that I had no father. I would argue that I did have a father and they would reply, "We haven't seen him." I would point to the fact that my dad's clothes were in my parents' closet, and they would counter that he had clothes there for the rare times that he would come by and spend the night. Since I was what you would consider a "daddy's boy", this made me angry, but I was comforted by the fact that it wasn't true. In my neighborhood, there were a few homes such as mine where the father and mother were under one roof and raising the children together. However, most homes were single-parent homes. Much of the devastating and negative aspects of our society can be traced back to broken homes.

When a young man has no father to look up to, he will find someone to fill that void. The person he chooses to fill that void is critical in determining the direction of his life. Many have chosen the wrong figure to admire and utilize as guidance in their lives. Sometimes, there is no one else around to consider. Therefore, it's easy for individuals in the business of illegal drugs to find young people to sell their products.

Sure, greed plays a factor and the allure of the finer things this world has to offer, but a huge factor driving many young people to engage in an act that destroys their communities is the void within them that exists due to a missing father. The burden of making ends meet financially falls onto the shoulders of these youth and they choose an illegal path to survive. What the youth doesn't realize is that going in is easy, but there are consequences once he or she enters the agreement and getting out is extremely hard.

Another thing that I observed in my environment, although not true for all, but enough to be somewhat common was that often when a girl is missing a father, she will search for the attention that she craves from her missing father. One of the saddest things I have seen are young girls and women repeatedly settling for guys who are clearly not worth their time, simply because he tells her he loves her, and he shows her more attention than she has received from any male figure in her life. Eventually, after receiving all that he wanted from the relationship, the guy is off to the next girl and many times he leaves behind a baby destined to grow up fatherless unless someone steps up to fulfill the role. It's a cycle that keeps going generation after generation. There was a significant need for more men to rise up and commit to breaking generational cycles of void regarding manhood, and to do so in Biblical form.

(3)

Environmental Challenges

DRUGS WERE ALSO part of the community. I saw how drugs destroyed people and I made up my mind to never do any drugs. While hanging out with a kid I knew, peer pressure got the best of me. I was bored, and he and his friends were the only ones to hang around with at the time. He passed a joint filled with marijuana to me and I began to smoke it. I expected some type of effect, but it had no effect on me. They were beyond high and extremely affected, but I didn't feel or experience anything. I thought, "this is stupid" and never did it again. Apparently, something was very wrong with the marijuana (perhaps it was laced with something). They became extremely sick. This was another time that God didn't allow the usual consequences to occur in my life.

The only other encounter I had with drugs was when a kid my age who had everything he wanted and plenty of money revealed to me why he was so financially stable. He showed me what he said was crack cocaine and by doing so he was unofficially offering me an opportunity to make some money. I looked at the tiny rocks and thought within myself, "this is what all of the hype is about?" Everyone that grew up in my generation had heard of crack cocaine. It completely changed the landscape of many urban, suburban and even some rural communities. Those who used crack were hooked to such a degree that there was nothing that they would not do to get it. I have seen individuals who were addicted to crack carry objects that normally required a couple of people to lift, single-handedly to destinations where they could sell the item and get money to fund their habit. Here, I was being offered an opportunity to join the ranks of those who distributed this weapon of mass destruction. I can't remember what I said to him, but I never took him up on his offer. I gradually began to stop hanging around him. Not to avoid him, but due to the fact he was busy heading in a direction I was not going, and I would only slow him down.

Gangs became a popular thing, and when you were associated with one of them, you had no fear of anyone giving you any problems unless it was another gang. Throughout the city, there were various gangs and it became hard to navigate around them. You offend one in the group and you now had a problem with the entire group. One day, a member of one of the gangs came to my house to play basketball and decided he wanted to leave with my ball. We had a small confrontation, and I tried to be smart and not do something that was significant enough to cause him to go and get his friends. At this time, basketball was everything to me. I was able to keep my basketball that day, but I wondered when I might run into problems because of it. While preparing to exit the bus at a local bus stop one day, I noticed the guy and the entire gang standing on a small hill next to the bus stop. I knew that I was in trouble, but there was a simple and easy solution to the problem: I could stay on the bus and ride it to the next stop and get off there. I didn't mind the fact that it would place me farther from home. Suddenly, I noticed my mother standing across the street near the gang. She had come to walk home with me, which never happened because I was too old for that. I had to get off the bus now. I knew that the gang would not care that my mother was around, and they would attack her too. I had previously seen another classmate within the neighborhood and his mother, get attacked while walking home. Not knowing what was about to happen, I exited the bus. As soon as I got off, someone nearby from a rival group shouted something to the gang and started to run. The gang began to chase him in the opposite direction of where I needed to go. I met my mother and walked home quickly.

These were just a few of the challenges I faced as I navigated through life in my environment. Each day presented both old and new challenges. These challenges have produced benefit. Because of my years of navigating various instances, I am usually very good at thinking quickly when in situations which require quick action. This is a skill I had no choice, but to develop growing up in Eldorado.

(4)

Basketball

THE ONE ADVANTAGE I had in my environment was that I was decent at playing basketball. I dunked a basketball for the first time when I was in the 6th grade. My father introduced me to the game. One day he bought me a basketball rim and we nailed it to a post in the backyard; from that moment on I was hooked. Eventually my father, being a welder, created an incredible basketball hoop and pole for me, and that intensified my passion for the game. I would watch basketball on TV for hours and then go outside and play for hours. My favorite player was Reggie Miller. I imitated him by practicing for lengthy periods of time on my three-point shot. Other boys in the neighborhood would come and play in my yard and many times some of those that came were from other neighborhoods around the city. I loved every minute of it. There were periods of time when we couldn't play at my house because someone went too far and dunked the ball hard enough to break the rim away from the backboard and my parents wouldn't fix it due to all the attention my homemade court was beginning to attract.

Eventually, they would always cave in and replace the rim and it was on again. The owner of the two-story, two-unit apartment building next door was not thrilled about the crowds in my yard, so they put up a thin wire fence to divide our yard and their property. It fulfilled its purpose in the beginning. However, eventually, a section of it got damaged and it simply failed to produce the results they were looking for. Those who came to play had absolutely no regard for the fence and trampled a section of it. I would attempt to fix it and try to persuade everyone to avoid it, but they never heeded the instruction.

Later, I discovered the local Boys & Girls Club. Many went there to play basketball and I became one of them. I wasn't the best basketball player, but I was far from being the worst. I had a feeling deep within me that there was no limit to where I could go with basketball if I worked hard and kept myself out of trouble. The game gave me a reason to stay off the streets and I spent a lot of my time working on my game. One day while playing at the Club, I stole the ball from a player on the opposing team and began to run quickly down the court with the ball toward my team's goal. My adrenaline was pumping so fast that I forgot about my human limitations. I leaped into the air slightly past the free throw line and hung in the air for what seemed like forever before dunking the ball. The gym went crazy and one of the club directors stopped the game and began to ask everyone if they had just seen that. To me, it was no big deal, but what I hadn't realized was that if I had jumped a few inches sooner I would have dunked from the free throw line, but I highly doubt that I could have dunked from that distance. Considering my age at the time, that was a very big deal.

I had a few people that wanted to help me develop my skills, but I was so unfocused. During this time, I wasted a lot of opportunities. I had the passion to play the game but working hard was not in my vocabulary. I was a very lazy kid. People would explain to me the potential that I had, but I couldn't see it; I failed to allow them to help me. On one occasion, a well-known individual who was experienced in basketball cursed at me as he expressed both anger and frustration with me. He knew my talent was very raw, but that I had potential if I would only let him help me. You may think, "what an awful way to act toward a kid," and your point is valid, but this man cared a lot for me and didn't want me to end up like so many others, who were dead, in prison, or in the streets. Although the subject was basketball, the purpose behind his plea was to save my life.

Another similar incident occurred during a physical education class in high school, although, this one was less dramatic. The boys' basketball coach walked into the gym just as I began flying through the air and dunking on those that came between me and the rim. His jaw dropped, he stopped the game and called me over to him. He asked me why I hadn't tried out for the school team. My reply was that I didn't know why I hadn't tried out for the team. But, I knew why. I couldn't play basketball, because my grades were not good enough. I was failing or just getting by in my classes. This would be an issue throughout most of my high school years.

One year, I was given an opportunity to try out for the team because my grades were right on the borderline of being acceptable. I was certain that I was going to make the team and that nothing was going to stand in my way. Every shot I took never went in during tryouts, not even easy layups. Dunking allowed all the other aspects of my game to become activated, but the coach was opposed to dunking during tryouts. To make matters worse, during shoot around one day I went up for a dunk in my usual manner but didn't jump high enough. When this occurs, there is the potential of getting "hung" on the rim, which consists of the individual attempting to slam the ball through the hoop but slamming it on the rim instead. The person attempting the dunk can fall or at best land on their feet and begin to stumble in an awkward manner. I fell flat on my back and it made the loudest sound imaginable. The gym exploded with laughter. The good thing is many of them knew that I could dunk so the jokes weren't too bad.

At the time, I knew something outside of myself was controlling the circumstances. There were times when I put the ball directly in the basket and it still came out. Years later, I reflected on that moment and realized God didn't allow the ball to go in because basketball was not His will for my life; He had other plans for me. I felt so low when I found out that I didn't make the team. Basketball was everything to me and I had blown it. When I look back on the experience, a Bible verse comes to mind: "Many are the plans in a person's heart, but it is the Lord's purpose that prevails," Proverbs 19:21, (NIV).

During the summer months, the Boys & Girls Club would have basketball leagues based on age groups. I played in the 16- to 18-year-old age group, and the games were incredible. The best basketball players in the city played in these leagues; if you could play basketball, you had to be there. The results of the games were published in the local newspaper the next day. It was an amazing feeling to see your name in the newspaper for basketball!

Ask anyone around at that time and they will tell you that the most talented players in the city were present in these games. Many could have achieved remarkable things, but most of us never reached our full potential in basketball. I had the desire but lacked the work ethic. I am one of those athletes who can only wonder about what could have been if I had only done things differently. In-spite of this, the game served a significant purpose by keeping me out of trouble.

(5)

The Desire for Freedom!

I THANK GOD for the values instilled in me at home because those values have kept me out of prison and the grave. I was never willing to go all the way with the negative plans of those I was with. When the events of the evening ventured into breaking the law, I said goodbye and headed home. The values I had been given wouldn't allow me to go as far as those around me were willing to go. I had been taught: "Do not be deceived: God cannot be mocked. A man reaps what he sows," Galatians 6:7, (NIV). The fear of God was in me, although I ignored that fear in many areas of my life. When I say "fear," I am not solely speaking of being afraid of God, but a level of reverence as well.

Deep down, I wanted to please God, but I didn't have the power to overcome temptation sometimes. However, He was still protecting me. I remember attempting to join a gang and the leader looked at me with a look that seemed to express, "you are not one of us." Not in a way that insinuates that I was incapable of doing what was required, but in a way, that seemed to say, "You have been chosen by someone greater." He simply said, "we'll see." I never received an opportunity to join. I couldn't have been good at that anyway. I respected my parents and I had a curfew when I was allowed to venture away from home. When things reached the level of criminality, you could count me out. I did however receive a pass and was able to hang out with members of the gang sporadically.

I wasn't allowed to hang out every night. School nights were certainly off the table. I used to be extremely sad when my mother refused to allow me to leave. My father was working long hours and I longed for him to be there because I thought he would understand my need to go and be with my friends. I longed for my mother to be like the mothers that allowed their kids to run the streets all night. I was permitted to go to a neighborhood friend's house a couple of blocks away or to any of the basketball spots during the week, but other opportunities only occurred on weekends. Although I was highly blessed to have my mother, I felt unfortunate at the time. I thought I was the unlucky one and many of the kids who had no father or no mother or those being raised by grandparents were lucky. They could go where they wanted, when they wanted and do whatever pleased them.

Over time, as I got older, I was allowed out more often and given greater freedom. My friends and I went to places that we should have never gone and hung out with people we should have never been with. I would tell my parents that I was heading to one place and I would, but my friends and I would leave that spot and head to various parts of the city.

I was always joking around. In the streets, being a comedian can get you killed. One night, I found this out in an almost tragic way. I was joking around with this man who may have been drunk or high. He said that someone had treated him very harshly and possibly took his money. I proceeded to treat the situation as a joke and made those around me laugh. I was with another guy who had to run off for a bit and then he returned. I didn't know he was related to the man I was making fun of. When the supposedly drunk or high man told the guy that I was with about the person who stole his money, they both went to retrieve the stolen money from the thief. The group of people standing around that night told me that I was lucky for not getting killed for what I did; the guy I was with would snap on me if he knew what I did to his relative. At that moment, I became very nervous because I knew that they were right. The issue was worked out with the person who took the money without any violence and the guy I was with came back and said, "let's go" and we hit the streets again.

I had a hunger for freedom and as I gained more freedom, I began to make bad choices. I had a flawed view of freedom. Freedom wasn't being out in the streets maneuvering from one spot to another. Freedom was being at home soaking up all the values and lessons I was taught so that one day I could head out into the world and apply those things and really soar. I was like a baby bird in a nest attempting to exit before I fully knew how to fly. That's dangerous!

One of the worst things I could ever imagine doing was disappointing my parents so that kept me from developing a lot of bad habits that many others developed. However, there were moments when the urge to do wrong was just too tempting to ignore. An example would be the moment when a friend came over in a nice new car and told me to hop in. I knew that he had no license and no money to buy a car, but I was bored, and I got into the car. The car belonged to the mother of a girl that he knew. The girl had lent the car to him for a few hours without her mother knowing and now I was riding with him. You would think that I would have gotten out of the car immediately after discovering this, but no. I wanted to drive, and he allowed me to do it. I was riding around the city in the car and I didn't have a driver's license.

I wasn't selling drugs, killing, or doing many of the other evil things I saw around me, but stupid decisions like the car incident threatened to ruin my future. I was at the door of becoming a grown man and I needed to make better decisions if I were going to have a bright future. As a result of my bad decisions, I was about to receive some devastating news.

(6)

You Can't Graduate!

SCHOOL WAS NOT a priority to me. By the time I had reached my junior year of high school, I had wasted so much time and neglected school to such a degree that a school counselor informed me that I would not graduate high school on time due to a lack of necessary credits. It wasn't my parent's fault. They had done everything they could to get me on the right track, but nothing had worked. I don't know how they had the patience to deal with it. I would bring bad grades home year after year and no matter how hard they tried, no matter what the consequences were, my grades never improved.

There were many factors that led to this. During my elementary school years, I was teased mercilessly because I had a lazy eye. It's hard to focus on your curriculum when the whole class is laughing at you. I was teased so badly that some wouldn't dare associate themselves with me for fear of becoming targets as well. When I first moved to El Dorado, I attempted to play sports on the school playground with the other kids to fit in, but I had never played sports before and I didn't know the rules. I remember a moment when I messed up so much during a football game that my team went ballistic, stopped the game, and kicked me off the team. All the boys were playing football and I had to spend the rest of the year sitting alone and watching them. Eventually I gravitated towards the class clown group. The kids were laughing at me anyway, so I might as well utilize it to produce some form of good. However, this role didn't help me to avoid all trouble.

One day in elementary school, a group of boys on the playground jumped me and beat me up in front of a substitute teacher. The first kid to approach me was not strong enough to take me out. I was swinging, and my punches were effective, but then the rest of them joined him. I was hurt badly in the incident. It was a miracle that I didn't get my neck broken, because one of the kids, who was very big and likely should have been in middle school instead of elementary school, lifted me above his head and another kid hit me with his forearm across my chest and stomach. I plunged to the ground, landing on my head and shoulder before being laid out flat on the ground. You would think that would be enough, but then they began punching, kicking, and stomping on me. The substitute teacher was very young, and I could see the fear on her face; she didn't know what to do or how to respond.

During this time groups began to form on the playground and if you were not a part of a group, which I wasn't, you were destined for trouble. I thought the whole group thing was stupid and decided to be independent and the consequence of doing so finally caught up with me. These early experiences shaped my total view of education. In my little mind at the time I realized school was a bad place with bad circumstances so to me education itself was bad.

Middle school was tough as well because, at that point, boys began liking girls and girls began liking boys. I had nice clothes, but they weren't of any popular brands and the kids would make fun of my clothes every day. One day, I discovered this nice brand name tracksuit with matching top and bottom that someone had given my mother for one of us to wear. I decided to wear it to school, although, I knew it was too small. At that time, tracksuits were very popular. Everyone would roll the lower leg sections of their pants up. Well, it was popular to roll only one of them up, but I decided I would roll both up and create a new trend because the pants didn't quite reach my ankles. I thought no one would notice the suit was too small. I also decided to roll the sleeves of the suit up to my elbows, because they didn't quite reach my wrists. Imagine me walking around school with both pants legs and sleeves rolled up. It worked at first, but as the day dragged on I got laughed off the face of the planet, because the legs accidentally slid down exposing the fact that the pants were too short. It's funny how today having pants that are too short is a fashion trend for guys. When I was growing up there were two things that your pants could not be and that is too short or too tight, but today it's popular amongst guys to do both.

In middle school, I would see a girl that I really liked, and she would end up liking my friend or some other dude. Few girls wanted a guy like me. On top of that, I had a lazy eye. My left eye drifted, making it impossible for me to look straight at anyone or thing. Many times, when I spoke to people they would ask, "are you talking to me?" Some asked out of sincerity and others out of an opportunity to crack some jokes. This was an issue I had for years until I was able to have my eye surgically corrected after I had become an adult. Class clown worked sometimes in middle school, but most of the time I would try to be incognito and not draw attention to myself. I also began to laugh when other kids were being teased and join in with those that were teasing them to keep me from becoming the subject of such attacks.

High school was different, there wasn't much teasing and my status improved enough for me to be comfortable. I sporadically had girlfriends. By this time, I had developed so many bad habits that I didn't know how to be a good student and do well. So, like I stated earlier I was informed that I wouldn't graduate because I didn't have enough credits. When my mother received the news that I wasn't going to graduate, it devastated her, but she refused to accept it. She had a meeting with the school counselors and arranged for me to spend my senior year of high school at an alternative school called Watson High School, which had a program for students in my circumstances.

The school was divided into two sections. The section I attended was designed for students who were struggling in school but had the potential to do well if they remained focused. The other section was for students who were one step away from juvenile or even adult prison. If we ever got into trouble, we would be sent to that other section, and none of us wanted that. So, the teachers never had problems with anyone in my section.

This school had a tremendously positive impact on me. For the first time in my life, I couldn't wait to go to school. I especially enjoyed it when we had visitors. Some of the visitors were brought in to give speeches or talk to us one-on-one about a wide range of topics. The visitors who had the greatest impact on me were former students who graduated and had gone on to become successful. When they would share their success stories, it showed me that there was hope and that I could be successful in life. I also had to volunteer in the community at a recreation center and at a food kitchen that served the poor and underprivileged. By helping others, I began to find purpose and I learned how fortunate I was.

At the food kitchen, I saw individuals that I went to school with come through for a meal. They appeared to be ashamed when they saw me, but I would do what I could to make them feel comfortable with coming in for what they needed. My schedule at this time was very structured and filled with things to do, which was what I needed. I didn't have time for the things that would get me into trouble.

During this time, I decided that I needed to get out of my environment. I didn't think I had the focus necessary to go to college and I didn't want to put that pressure on my parents financially. My sister was extremely smart and did very well in school. I knew she would be going to college and my parents would have to pay for it; she deserved it far more than I did. I also had a little brother who would eventually need to go to college too and that would be even more financial responsibility for my parents. I knew that I would never make it if I stayed in my hometown. After considering my situation, I chose to join the United States Army.

(7)

Becoming a Soldier

FOUR DAYS AFTER graduating high school, I stood face to face with a man who was yelling at me and shouting commands. In my hometown, you never allowed someone to speak to you in this manner, but I was no longer in that setting. I was in Army boot camp and there was no way that I was going to mess up this opportunity. I complied with every command given to me and I relied heavily on God to get me through the experience.

There was no greater feeling than seeing my parent's faces, painted with pride as they watched me graduate Army basic training. After enduring nine weeks of intense physical and mental discipline, I had made it. I felt as though there was nothing in this world that I couldn't conquer. I relished that moment for as long as I possibly could, knowing it would be short-lived. Soon, I would be off to Gulfport, Mississippi for Advanced Individual Training (AIT) where I would then study to become an engineer.

AIT school was much harder for me than basic training. When I joined the Army, I was given one of two options. I could either choose my job, letting the Army decide where I would go; or, the Army would choose my job, allowing me to decide on the location. A wintry weather climate was not an option for me. So, the Army chose engineer and I choose Hawaii.

After arriving, I soon discovered that many of my fellow students in AIT already had previous engineering experience, even if it was basic. I was completely new to the field and it didn't take long before I was falling behind. However, failure was not an option. I forced myself to work twice as hard. In the classroom, the instructors were given full control over students. Outside training hours, we were handed back over to our drill sergeants. I thought one drill sergeant, in particular, was totally against me and hated me. Today I realize why she had been so strict with me. It was the only way to successfully get me through training.

I had tremendous issues with my knees, which led to occasional visits to see a medical specialist. These trips to the doctor's office caused me to miss class often. Finally, my doctor explained to me that a growth spurt had been the reason behind my frequent pain. Evidently, my body was still in the process of growing. Due to the frequency of my visits, I was granted permission to see my doctor unaccompanied by my drill sergeants.

While leaving an appointment one day, I remembered hearing that there was a pay phone inside a beauty shop that I was just coming up to. I walked inside eager to call some of my friends back home. I thought no one would ever catch me there. Then, mid-conversation, in walked the drill sergeant I mentioned previously. It was her day off and she had an appointment there. "What exactly do you think you're doing?" she said, "Explain yourself, soldier!" With no valid answer to her question, I took off running as fast as I could. I lost all my special privileges from that point going forward. While everyone else enjoyed their well-deserved time off base each weekend, I was left alone in the barracks. It seemed as though she was always around to correct me on every little mistake. Yet, if I were to run into her today I would thank her. She taught me discipline. I didn't understand it then, but now I see the importance of having someone like her in my life at that time.

Soon came the last opportunity during our training to go out and enjoy the weekend. To my surprise, the drill sergeant still ordered me not to leave the barracks. I didn't understand. I had learned from my mistake and hadn't done anything wrong since. Looking back on that moment now, I could see that she was still attempting to protect me from myself. While sitting there alone in my barracks, a different drill sergeant stopped by and noticed me sitting at the end of my bunk.

"Why aren't you out having a good time with everyone else?" he asked. "Believe me, staying here was not my choice," I clarified before going on to explain how I had been restricted to the barracks since losing my off-base privileges. "Well," he hesitated. I could tell by the look on his face he felt sorry for me. "Go on, get out of here soldier!" He didn't have to tell me twice. Before I could think of what my first drill sergeant had instructed, I grabbed what I could and ran with the wind.

I called up my fellow training buddies telling them I was a free man. They gladly provided me with the address of the hotel where their festivities would continue to take place. I had an absolute blast that weekend! However, I had discovered the activities that took place before arriving at the hotel were legal, but not good. I couldn't help thinking if I were there instead of locked in the barracks, I would have made some bad mistakes? This was unmistakably a sign from God; He was protecting me from myself by not allowing me to go out on those previous weekends. This final weekend was very mellow and chill.

Graduation day eventually came at the end of my training. The class would be seated based on each individual's grade point average. The student with the top score would be seated first while the lowest scoring student would be sat last. I graduated at the bottom of my class. That last seat was reserved for me. I was devastated, but at least I had made it. Next stop, Hawaii.

(8)

Living in Paradise

HAWAII IS TRULY the most beautiful place I have ever seen. I can't imagine how beautiful Heaven must be if a place here on Earth can look so wonderful. The beauty of the island also came with many temptations. Upon arrival, I was placed in a temporary, in-processing Army unit on a base called Schofield Barracks. I immediately became friends with a guy who was also new to the base but had been there for a week. He had bought a nice sports car so the following evening, he and I left the base and were on our way to Honolulu. We were headed towards a place I had only heard about, but never experienced — the club.

We hit up one of the local clubs and it was everything I had ever imagined it to be. I was loving every second of it. After a long night of partying, my new friend and I tried making our way back to base, but we couldn't remember how to get back. This may seem silly today, but back then GPS technology was not as prevalent as it is today. By the time we figured it out, the sun was starting to rise, leaving us with just enough time to get dressed and report to my first-morning formation.

Army life was great, but it also came with its hardships. Being thousands of miles away from family back home was difficult for me. The arduous work of an engineer was laborious when we had projects going on. While joining the Army, I had wanted to become a military policeman, but I gave that up when I chose Hawaii as my duty station. I still wouldn't change a thing. I met a lot of great people inside my engineering unit who made each day worth it. I considered my military comrades to be as close as a biological brother or sister. Some of them remain my close friends to this day.

My newly developed level of self-discipline led to almost no incidents between me, and my sergeants. I never received any form of discipline or negative counseling statement for the remainder of my time in the Army. During this time, my closest friends were either married or had long-time girlfriends whom they spent most of their time with. My path was a little different. I went on dates and met several girls, but none of them seemed to inspire me to take it any further than a date or they weren't looking to be with any one specific and were just testing the waters of possibility.

While I knew I was lost and had no relationship with God, I knew I still wanted a Godly woman. If a girl was not interested in placing her faith in Jesus Christ as I had planned to do some day, I wouldn't pursue a relationship. This reveals the flaws of my thinking at the time. Tomorrow isn't guaranteed to anyone. I could have easily died in my sins. It was arrogant to think that I could just one day say, "Ok, now I'm ready." There were, of course, a few exceptions when I knew I should have left a girl alone but tried to move forward anyway. Every time this occurred, the situation would dissolve somehow, and it would leave me baffled and asking; what just happened? It seemed as though I was being protected from making the wrong choice.

I had joined the Army as a virgin and was set on riding myself of that title. My first opportunity came with a beautiful girl. Together we had a nice, innocent outing and had it ended at that, the night would have turned out great, but that night I lost my virginity. My father had warned me as a teenager, that once I had made the mistake of having sex outside of marriage it would be the beginning of an addictive and dangerous habit. That's exactly what happened. Once I committed my first act, I had to repeat it.

Eventually, I met a girl who happened to be a stripper at a local gentlemen's club. During my time in the Army, I only went to a place like this once. I thought it was the most stupid thing I'd ever witnessed. Men were giving women money to dance before them. After a few minutes, the woman would walk away richer leaving the man with temporary gratification and less money. It wasn't for me.

This girl was different than the others in this environment. She was nice and demanded respect. I never understood why she did what she did, especially when she also had a regular day job. Maybe the day job wasn't enough. Despite her occupation, over time we really enjoyed each other's company. I would drop her off at the club, and come back later when her shift ended, and drive her home. When guys would follow and harass her outside the club, she'd quickly jump into my car knowing I would get her out of there quickly. I learned that woman who worked in these places attracted stalkers consistently. It's a really scary environment once you have an opportunity to see how it all works behind the projected scene.

One night she came to visit, and I started to take things a little further than normal, but I suddenly decided not to go all the way, and things became different between us. We stopped seeing each other as much and eventually lost all communication. I'm not sure why the friendship ended. I guess we might have simply drifted apart from one another. Some good did come from our short friendship; I later saw her, and she told me that she had quit her job at the strip club. Maybe the conversations we shared led to that. Or, maybe me treating her like a lady instead of an opportunity triggered something within her, changing her mindset on life.

I had become friends with a couple of guys in the Army whom many would consider "ladies' men." By hanging out with them, opportunities to meet girls were automatic. During the few occasions, when I would bring a girl home with me, we spent the night talking and nothing sexual happened. I wasn't looking for quick fulfillment. I wanted something more than lust. I wanted to find the perfect girl to settle down and spend the rest of my life with. My interest was in getting to know someone through conversation and time spent together.

On one occasion however, there was no talking because she and I were on the same page. A friend of mine had to drive to another section of the island of Oahu to pick up a girl he had met. This girl also had a friend she wanted to bring along; therefore, I was needed to accompany the three of them. The moment I laid eyes on this girl the trip became well worth it.

We brought the girls back to the base where my buddy and his date went to his room and I went to mine with my date. Just when she and I were about to take things too far, there was a lot of banging on my door. I thought, "Maybe some of the other guys in the barracks saw me bring a girl home." I figured it was them, joking around. I quickly got up to open the door and saw my buddy's girl. She looked frantic and wanted to go home immediately.

I began thinking something horrible happened between her and my friend. Seconds later he too came running in breathing heavily. After talking amongst themselves, the girls said they would meet us out at the car. My buddy was devastated having driven all the way to the other side of the island only for his girl to have second thoughts on what they had agreed to do. Disappointment filled the car during the ride back to their neighborhood. Not one word was spoken among us. Another moment of intervention to add to the many others that had occurred. This was typical of life in Hawaii for me. Adulthood didn't seem so bad. If I was able to get through the workday, all was well.

1982

Elementary School
198?

Picture was taken hours before
my high school graduation.

Army basic training photo.

Living in paradise. (Hawaii)

Training

Leaving the war and heading home.

First photo taken after returning to America.

Acting – Freedom Stage Play by Coffy Davis

Sharing my testimony.

(9)

Lost and Found

I ENJOYED OCCASIONAL trips to local clubs, but I never made it a weekly thing like some. The minimum goal was to leave the club with the phone number of a young lady that peaked my interest. There were however, the random nights when the liquid courage of alcohol running through me sometimes aimed for more. I remember one occasion in which I was successful in this and the way I handled the situation is regrettable.

I met a girl at a club who was on vacation and while nothing happened that night, on the following night we ended up going all the way without any interruptions. I could tell she really liked me and saw a probable future with me and I liked her as well. We spent a few more nights together before she eventually had to fly back to her home. The distance killed the communication. I could have made a greater effort but didn't. A couple years later I was fortunate enough to have an opportunity to apologize for my lack of effort and for that I am grateful.

I was a compulsive liar and quite talented at it. I would lie about all types of things. My words were so convincing people completely believed me without question. The lies had escalated to the point where I couldn't remember fact from fiction. I couldn't be trusted. I couldn't promise anyone anything. My word had become worthless. I was lost and needed to get a grip on myself. One day I went out and bought myself a Bible and read the entire New Testament beginning to end. Truthfully, I didn't comprehend much of what I read, but at least I was trying.

I was sitting in my barracks room one day when a girl stopped by and came into my room. She invited me to a church service being held by an evangelist who was only going to be on the island for a couple of days. Her friend would be coming with us also. Inside the church, the preacher was speaking, and I began to feel as though something great was going to happen. That night was going to be my breakthrough moment, but then the girl who had invited me suddenly said it was time to head home, so we left before the preacher had an opportunity to get into his sermon. Later that same night a different girl approached me with an entirely different opportunity. Her temptations were hard, but I overcame them.

I needed a miracle from God. I wanted to change and start living for him, except, I didn't know how. I didn't have the capability of changing myself, and I needed to be changed. In desperation, I wrote a small note to God asking that He save me. I placed the note in the middle of my Bible. I continued to stumble and fall, but God was about to show up in my life in a way I could never have predicted.

I was partying with friends in Honolulu and afterward, they'd decided on renting out a hotel room for the night. I had also decided not to drive all the way back to the base, so I decided to stay with them at the hotel. Like everyone else I slept where there was open space. I found a clear spot on the floor and fell asleep. I suddenly woke up from a deep sleep and immediately realized I was extremely sick; something was wrong. I felt as if all the strength within me had been replaced with a terrible weight. I rushed around trying to find my shoes and car keys. "Yo, where you going?" One of my friends asked. "I don't feel good. I'm going to try and make it to a hospital," I answered. He fell back to sleep probably too disoriented to realize what I had just said. I drove to the Tripler Army Medical Center and checked myself into the emergency room.

For the next couple of months, my condition continued to decline. Looking back, I don't know how I managed to survive. I could hardly eat. I used the last bit of energy I had left going to different medical professionals all unable to find any evidence of what was going on. Eventually, they all started to believe I was faking my symptoms. No matter how hard I tried to explain my excruciating symptoms, no one seemed to understand the gravity of what I was experiencing. I didn't know it at the time, but this was God's doing. He was taking away all other options leaving nothing except the choice to turn to Him.

The work of an engineer became harder and harder until the required physical strength was unbearable. Thinking I was about to die, I requested a thirty-day leave and bought a plane ticket back home to Arkansas. My mother took me to a medical facility at Little Rock Air Force Base. They too were unable to find a reason for my suffering. I returned to my parents' home where I seemed to just fade away.

Nearing the end of my thirty days leave, there was no way that I could have made it back to Hawaii. My mother invited me to a church convention. I agreed to go despite being very sick. As I listened to the minister deliver his message at the convention, reality began to set in. I could feel my time here on Earth coming to an end. I knew I was leaving this world. Knowing you're about to die goes beyond any normal feeling. It was more like entering into a more real reality. I could have easily asked any of the people around me to call an ambulance, but I knew that it was pointless to do so. It didn't even enter my mind to do that. I knew it was my time to go.

I thought to myself, "If only the minister would end his sermon and give an invitation to accept Jesus as Lord and Savior." If I was going to die at any moment, I wanted to do so after placing my faith in Jesus. At the time, I didn't know you could do that all on your own, without the invitation of a minister.

So many times, during my life I had sat through many church services with the Holy Spirit urging me to go forward and accept His invitation, to place my faith in Jesus Christ. Many times, I wanted to, but I was too shy to show such vulnerability to an entire church full of people and lacked the understanding that I could do so outside of a church service also. Now, here I was at the end of my life hoping for one more opportunity in an arena filled with over a thousand people. "Please, just one more invitation!" I cried out to God within myself.

The minister ended his sermon and invited those who were ready to accept Jesus Christ as Lord and Savior to come forward, near the stage. Where the energy came from? I don't know, but I ran towards the stage as though my life depended on it and accepted Jesus as Lord and Savior. Others began coming forward to-

wards the stage also, including my sister. God saved
me that night and He healed my body. I was ecstatic! I
was saved. I was now a believer! "But, Now what?
Where do I go from here?"

(10)

Conviction

ONE OF THE worse things to ever happen to me was when a childhood friend gave me a VHS tape containing pornography. Pornography is a destructive tool Satan uses to destroy many minds. Countless men and women have fallen in this destructive trap, ruining relationships, marriages, careers and more. Pornography is as addictive as any drug, enslaving those who allow it into their lives. Including me.

Even before watching the tape, I had seen brief glimpses of sexual immorality. I saw it in the relationships around me and throughout my childhood community. Also, as a small child, on a few occasions, girls my age and older had shown me their private parts, so the seeds had already been planted.

As parents, it's critical that we monitor exactly what our children are exposed to including what they view on television, computers and phones. My home life consisted of living a lifestyle based on Biblical principles. My parents would never allow me to watch something capable of tainting my mind. The rules were sometimes more relaxed in some of the households of my friends within my neighborhood growing up. There I would be introduced to content I would have never had access to in my own home. This exposure at such an early age was the beginning of a sickening habit that followed me into adulthood.

Growing up adults offered me pornography despite my adolescence. I never felt comfortable taking it, except for one occasion. The individual didn't exactly offer it to me, but they kept pornography within their home in the form of magazines. One day, they had caught me looking through the pages and hadn't said anything or at the least bit tried to stop me. Eventually, guilt got to them and the magazines were eradicated.

Although pornography was everywhere, my experiences were never allowed to last too long. Whatever the source was, it would eventually become unavailable somehow. Much like the magazines, the friend who had offered me the original VHS tape had a change of heart and stopped letting me borrow them after a few times. After that, I couldn't get my hands on the material until I was a grown man out on my own.

Today, pornography can be accessed at the palm of your hand using any device capable of connecting to the internet. Back in the 1990's and early 2000's pornography was only available in limited forms such as printed magazines, VHS tapes, and eventually DVD's. I tried to keep my habit a secret in the Army, but occasionally the urge would drive me to borrow DVD's from others around me.

There was an adult only store located near the base where you could acquire a wide range of sex-related items, including pornography. I went into it once, but it was too close to base for me to feel comfortable going into it. I eventually found a store further off base. I didn't want to risk possibly running into someone I knew. Conviction and shame only allowed me to go into that store a couple of times.

After my conversion and healing experience

conviction dealt a significant blow to my engagement with pornography and when I would engage it something would occur to keep me from really indulging in it as much as I wanted to. Around this time, I met a girl. She had a heart for God and was active in her local church. She was another blow to my pornography habit. I thought my time spent with her and the zeal she had for God would put me on the right track, but the greatest help in overcoming my areas of weakness came from the conviction I had started to feel when I did wrong. When I would purposely do wrong, I would no longer feel consciously free about doing so.

Before meeting my girlfriend, I had found a church although, their teachings played upon one's emotions instead of the Bible. On one occasion the pastor said anyone he touched would be blessed with thousands of dollars. Everyone, including me, were eager to receive the favor he claimed to be giving. One day the congregation was told not to give coins in the offering plate, only green money was accepted at this church. I didn't stay there very long. It wasn't a good place to be.

I found another church and placed my membership there. It was a Bible believing, Bible teaching church, but they lacked the community aspect of the faith. I only spoke with or saw any of the members on Sunday or at the weekly Bible study. I needed discipleship, but it wasn't available. No one reached out to me to see where I was in my walk with Christ or to even get to know me. Church was just a checklist item for the week. Although I remained an active member at this church, I sporadically started going with my girlfriend to her church.

As I spent more time with my girlfriend, life seemed relatively perfect. I was a very weak Christian who had no clue what he was doing as far as walking with Jesus and there was no one reaching out to me at the time to help me learn how to walk with Him. Looking back, I can see how I was a bad influence in some aspect on her life. Eventually, the day came where she ended our relationship. She was confused, and so was I at the time. In hindsight I can now see that it just wasn't meant to be. I still couldn't ignore how perfect this girl was and how she inspired me to be a better person. We eventually got back together and after a brief period we became engaged to get married.

Later, the relationship ended again. This time it was by my own doing. I kicked myself repeatedly afterwards for ending the relationship. I regretted that decision for years afterwards. Several years later I found out that she had gotten married and eventually had a child. This felt like a direct punch to the gut. Again, I was asking myself why I let her go. Why had I ended things with the woman I should have married? Suddenly, I heard an answer. "It was the Holy Ghost that led you to end it." Suddenly, I realized that it was not me who had ended the relationship. It was God. There was someone else meant for her and someone else meant for me.

I started making attempts to draw near to God, but I would become distracted and make costly mistakes. When this occurred, He would be there to guide me through it, whether I wanted him to or not. When I wanted to turn back to pornography all my sources of it were destroyed and my options eliminated. A television would stop working or the DVD player would malfunction. When I tried to connect with women that had no heart for God, I'd fail to get close or be allowed to go as far as I wanted, due to the circumstances somehow being orchestrated towards the elimination of whatever connection there was.

There were moments of falling and failing in various areas, but through each setback I began to change. I became content spending quiet nights alone at home instead of going out and doing things I shouldn't, and I continued going to church regularly. I even attempted to engage in evangelism for the first time by sharing my faith with an Army buddy and convincing him to attend a church service with me. His actions however, had me thinking he'd had a drink before going, which he was prone to do. Visitors were given the chance to introduce themselves during a portion of the service. When the time came, my buddy stood up, eyes squinted, and swayed and motioned with his right arm outstretched. He introduced himself as "Big Mike" from back east and ended his greeting with: "Man y'all know what it is." It left everyone puzzled, but that was Mike. This was totally within character for him.

Satan continued to fight hard trying to get me back on the wrong path. We moved from the barracks on base, into apartment style housing while the old barracks were demolished and re-built. Two of us shared one place and each had their own bedroom. Girls from various areas on base started coming to my room to watch movies and talk without me making any effort to get them to come over. Each day or night that this occurred, nothing sexual ever happened between us, even when the occasional opportunity was clearly there.

I once had a girl come over and it was clear that she had the wrong intentions. I was able to resist her agenda, but she refused to leave. Eventually she gave up and exited the apartment. On another occasion a girl tried to enter my place and I tried closing the door, but she would block it each time. To make matters worse, a second girl joined in to force the door back open. Eventually I was able to get the door to close and I immediately utilized the locks on it! I jokingly tell people that I am only 25% beautiful. I have never been a muscular guy or possessed the attributes that woman craved. With that being said, I know without any doubt these encounters were a work of our enemy the Devil. Overcoming in such circumstances was challenging, but I was resisting the temptation and trying do the right thing.

The mistake I was making at the time was allowing the girls to come to my room in the first place. In hindsight, I can now see this clearly, but at the time I was failing to see the mistake that I was making. I am grateful for the conviction that didn't allow me to go as far as I could have and would have gone before. I was however about to override conviction and it would almost cost me my life.

I was spending a quiet night at home watching a movie when a friend dropped by and asked me to go with him to a local club to celebrate his birthday. After refusing his offer several times he then asked if I would at least be his designated driver since he planned on drinking. I eventually caved in to his request. I hadn't been to a club in quite some time. Now I was back in an old environment and it was not as pleasant as it had seemed in times past. While at the club a major fight broke out. Fighting wasn't uncommon, but this fight was bigger and appeared to be much more dangerous. I had to avoid getting entangled in the mayhem or being mistaken as one of the brawlers by the club's bouncers. Somehow my friend and I made it out of the building only to see that the fighting had spread to the parking lot. We went to the car immediately and left the property as fast as we could. I drove around Honolulu trying to find a different club, so my friend could continue celebrating. It wasn't long before we both agreed to call it a night and head back to the base.

On the freeway, we encountered the same groups from the club now fighting on the left side of the freeway. The truck in front of me slowed down almost coming to a complete stop. Meanwhile the traffic to my right was still traveling at seventy miles an hour. Unable to slow down fast enough, or drift over into another lane, I crashed into the back of the truck in front of me. I was dazed at first, not knowing what had just happened. I only snapped back to reality when I heard someone yell, "Get out of the car! It's about to blow up!" I scrambled to get out as fast as I could. The car had been destroyed. I was shocked to see neither of us had visible injuries. I felt terrible, having wrecked my friend's vehicle.

The crash caused those who were fighting to quickly flee the scene. Thankfully the man in the truck that I hit wasn't hurt either. The incident scared me so bad I immediately called my dad to tell him what happened. I was embarrassed having wrecked the vehicle while being the designated driver; I felt even worse knowing that I had totaled my buddy's car. On top of all that, I had to fight just to keep my driver's license. My friend had to sign a form stating he would not be suing me for wrecking his vehicle so that no charges were filed against me and to keep my license from being suspended. I had never wanted to go out to the club that night, but I caved in and failed to heed conviction and it nearly cost me my life.

Around this time, one of my biggest mistakes was not forming close relationships with other Christians. I attended church, but it wasn't unlike me to miss a service. I didn't have any other Christian friends or leaders to hold me accountable for my actions or to simply walk me through the discipleship process. I was trying to do everything on my own without others there to encourage me.

I was also very shy around other Christians. I didn't speak up or know how to be social in a church environment. This led to a tendency to be secluded and withdrawn. I was a small lamb just wondering around in the designated pasture; sometimes ending up outside mingling with the wolves. Despite all of this, my Shepherd (Jesus) had His eyes on me and He was protecting me.

(11)

War

I HAD JOINED the Army in the year 2000. I knew going to war was a possibility, of course, but never did I think that I would be deployed to go fight in one. At that time, there were no major conflicts involving the United States. The country was at peace, and we were having a lot of fun in the military with no wars on the horizon. We trained hard and prepared for war, but it seemed more fantasy than an imminent reality.

September 11th, 2001, I woke up in the early hours of the morning before the sun was up. There were shouts and screams outside my window. Two of my fellow army buddies were yelling, "we're going to war" over, and over again. I remember thinking to myself, "these dudes must be drunk." I attempted to go back to sleep, but I felt there may have been some truth to what they were saying. What if they weren't drunk, but stating a fact? Abandoning my efforts to go back to sleep, I decided to turn on the television and flip to the news. By the time I found the channel the two World Trade Center towers had fallen in New York City. I didn't know that planes had been flown into them at first. All I saw was a massive heap of rubble and smoke, curling high into the air.

My initial thought was that someone had launched a missile at the city. I asked myself, "Who would do this? Who would attack us?" Then I saw the replays of the planes flying into the buildings. The horror of the moment was beyond words for me as I watched it all being replayed repeatedly on the screen in front of me. My phone suddenly rang, and I was instructed to report to my company headquarters immediately in uniform. Playtime was over. From this moment on, I was entering an entirely new, reality. Our company commander gave us a very sobering speech and from that moment on, we were preparing for war knowing that there was tremendous possibility that we would be deployed.

I thought we would be deployed within the near future, but that didn't happen. When the war in Afghanistan began, I was watching it on my television screen. It was sobering to see the images of the conflict on TV. The first hard reality that hit me after the war started was notification that I received regarding another soldier who had been in my unit. He had left Hawaii and went to another unit elsewhere. He was killed in combat. Having known someone, and to know that he died in such a way brings the reality of war crashing down on you.

I watched the beginning of the war in Iraq on television as well, but I eventually learned towards the end of 2003 that I would soon be deployed to Iraq for one year. On the day we were to leave, boyfriends said goodbye to girlfriends, girlfriends said goodbye to boyfriends, Husbands said goodbye to wives, wives said goodbye to husbands, fathers and mothers said goodbye to their children. The children were either heartbroken, confused or completely oblivious to the gravity of the moment depending on what age they were at the time. I had no one to say goodbye to. I had no girl-friend, wife, or family present that day. I simply watched as many others around me said goodbye to each other.

We made a few stops along the way, but we eventually arrived in the nation of Kuwait. We were to be briefed and prepared before we entered Iraq. We trained every day. The tension was high during these times, but we still found ways to enjoy ourselves. I enjoyed the time that I spent in Kuwait.

Eventually, the day came when it was time to head into Iraq. I would be driving one of the Humvees, which came as no surprise to me. I had a lot of experience driving. I had always been selected to drive. I drove on training missions, transported, picked up, dropped off, and I was once selected to be my commander's driver for a year. Now it was time to put all that experience to the test. The command was given to drive forward, and my heart started beating a little faster. I took a deep breath and went forward.

Iraq wasn't too bad the first two or three months. I remember thinking to myself, "This is easy. I can do this for a year." We were kept busy to keep us out of mischief, and it was a blessing. An idle mind is the worst thing to have in our unfamiliar environment. Eventually, the tides began to turn in Iraq, and we were getting attacked frequently. I lived in a camp called Anaconda, near the city of Balad. The camp was attacked daily with mortars and rockets.

One day we were working in an open area of the camp and the mortar rounds began to hit areas of the camp not far from us. I knew at any moment a mortar round could land where we were working. There was a building in the distance, and we started running towards it. We were fortunate, none of the mortars fell near us. When mortar rounds hit, they explode with an incredible burst of force, and anyone within a 50-yard radius is within the "kill zone," and anyone within double that distance is still in harm's way. I remember on another occasion, I had walked to a store on the camp to purchase some hygiene necessities. Mortar rounds began to hit just outside the building, and it seemed to shift and tremble every time a round hit. I will never forget the face of a lady who was standing near me. She had come to Iraq to work as a civilian contractor. The horror on her face gave voice to the feelings she could not vocalize at that moment. She was dressed in civilian clothing, no different than what she would wear if she were back in America and had no protective gear on. It wouldn't do much for me, but at least I had on a helmet and frag vest. After exiting the building, I could see all the damage done by the mortars. I was fortunate to have been inside when they began falling in the area.

Church services were held in a modern theatre on the camp each Sunday. I decided to attend. They had a choir, and I was told they rehearsed on a specific day each week. If I wasn't out on a mission, I was at the rehearsal every week going forward. This was the greatest fellowship experience I have ever had. It was far more than a simple rehearsal for me. We sang to the glory of God with completely pure hearts. We were at war and the horrible things we had to face and endure left our souls in desperate need of the only hope available to mankind: Jesus Christ. We were suffering, and each time we gathered, it was as if Christ entered the tent that we rehearsed in and began to comfort us. He understood our suffering. We were enduring so much hardship, so much tragedy and loss and fear, and He was comforting us the whole way through.

We laughed, cried, and comforted one another. We would each give testimonies of what God had done for us since we last met. Tremendous stories of God's grace were shared: near-death experiences, times God comforted individuals as they saw death and destruction around them. When we would sing on Sundays, before a full theatre of people, the Holy Spirit would elevate our worship to incredible heights. One time, we sang Richard Smallwood's song "Total Praise." Never have I heard something so beautiful as the sound created through us that day. It was Heavenly, and like nothing I had ever heard before. Everyone was deeply moved after that. I find myself fighting back tears even now, thinking back on this time in my life. I was in the middle of chaos, but I had total peace. At that moment, I felt no fear, only the Glory of God.

In May of 2004, we were given a mission that would require us to drive from Camp Anaconda to Kuwait and then back to Camp Anaconda. I was promoted to the rank of sergeant the day before we left. With that promotion came an even greater weight of responsibility for me to bear. We left Camp Anaconda and drove to a prison somewhere outside of Baghdad. We spent the night there. Inside, there was this giant mural of Saddam Hussein depicted in a crime boss/gangster type of way. It was weird seeing such an image in a place where prisoners were kept. The next morning, we began to exit the prison compound in our vehicles. Suddenly, a car crashed into one of the lead vehicles. My immediate thought was that a suicide bomber had tried to attack us, but it turned out to be just someone driving too fast. The vehicle was heavily damaged, but the decision was made for the remainder of the convoy to push on.

There was a staff sergeant on the convoy with me. He was a tough man, but deeply caring, and if he was your friend, you had a real friend. He and I had some great conversations. He was the most vocal person to congratulate me when I was promoted to sergeant. During the trip, we pulled off the road to refuel our vehicles, and he and I began to talk as we always did. He began to jokingly tell me that it was time for me to settle down and get married. When the conversation ended, I began walking back to the driver side of my vehicle to get in and prepare to move on. I can vividly remember seeing him looking into the distant horizon while eating sunflower seeds after I had begun to walk away. That image is burned into my memory permanently.

We began to push forward. Our convoy was massive and had over 30 vehicles in it. We eventually started to enter a town and immediately, calls came in over the radio that the vehicles at the beginning of the convoy had begun to take gunfire from each side of the road. It wasn't long after this news that the bullets began to hit my vehicle as well. I won't go into much detail of the events that occurred next, out of respect for the families of those we lost that day and respect for those with me that day, but at the end of this incident, the staff sergeant and another great soldier had been killed. During the incident I had seen a disabled Army vehicle on the side of the road. I began to slow down a little so that when I reached the vehicle, I would be able to see if anyone was still inside, but a higher-ranking sergeant in the vehicle with me said, "They would not have left them stranded, the vehicle behind them would have picked them up. Let's go. It made perfect sense to me logically. I thought for sure no one would have driven past them after seeing their vehicle become disabled, but the experience was extremely chaotic. As I passed the vehicle, I couldn't see any movement, but what I didn't realize is that two solders that belonged to a different unit that was traveling with us were still inside of the vehicle. Once we made it outside the town, we discovered that the two soldiers were missing. An effort to go back for them began but was not allowed to go forth. The two soldiers escaped the town in such a dramatic way that their story could be made into a movie. To this day, I still bear the regret of not doing more to ensure they never had to endure such a traumatic experience. I can only hope to one day have an opportunity to apologize to them both.

After this harrowing event, we eventually made it to a British camp. We had been through a tremendously hard encounter, and I couldn't even begin to process what I had just experienced. Before I could even get my bearings, the camp was attacked with mortar rounds. We hit the floor of the large dining facility tent we were in and then ran for a bunker outside that was designed to withstand this type of attack. We made it to the bunker, which was swelteringly hot with all the people huddled and crammed inside of it.

The next day I went back to my vehicle and began to count the marks made by the bullets. I gave up on counting because there were too many to count. I had to jump back into that same vehicle and drive to Kuwait. Along the remainder of the journey, my heart was heavy, and I was extremely alert. It felt like an attack was imminent every minute of the drive. We pressed forward through several nerve-racking areas, but we suffered no further attacks.

It was a huge relief to finally arrive in Kuwait. We were forced to go through mandatory counseling, but I wasn't prepared for it. Several times I thought about standing up and walking out. During this counseling session, I experienced what it is like to lose your mind. The gravity of what I had been through began to take its toll on me. I felt my sanity being snatched from me. Each time I felt this, I would say within myself, "Jesus."

When I called His name, it was as if the force that was tugging on my sanity would let go, and I gained the strength and the resolve I needed to hold onto my sanity. The tugging and my calling on Jesus occurred several times, and from that point forward, I knew beyond any doubt that my strength was in Jesus. He heard me, and He helped me. It reminds me of Psalm 116:1, which states, "I love the Lord, for he heard my voice, he heard my cry for mercy, (NIV)." The moment I cried out to Him, He heard me and saved me.

The counseling session ended, and we now had to travel back to Camp Anaconda. I really wasn't up for this trip. I knew it was what I had to do. Some of us would fly back and others would have to drive back. As hard as I try, I can't remember if I drove back or flew back. My mind seems to have erased the memory. I do remember that it was sobering to return to Camp Anaconda without all of those who had made the journey with us. We attended a ceremony to honor those we lost, and then we had to do all that we could to get back to the mission at hand.

(12)

The Return Home

DESPITE THE WONDERFUL experiences I encountered during the choir rehearsals and the Sunday services. I began experiencing some significant falls spiritually. Outside of those rehearsals and services I had no interaction with Christians, because no one around me was a follower of Jesus. With no accountability or discipleship mentors, I started caving in to various temptations. The climax of my failures consisted of a moment in which I went to an area of the camp where a girl who was also in the military lived. I shared an open space with several guys where I lived, but she had her own private quarters. We watched a movie together and afterwards things began to go too far, but I had to stop. I left and never made another visit.

Shortly after this occurred, I was allowed to take two weeks of R&R, (rest and relaxation). For two weeks, I was permitted to go wherever I wanted. I chose to go home to Arkansas to see my family. I had grown so used to a chaotic environment that I had completely forgotten what it was like to be in a normal one. I arrived back home in South Arkansas in early July. I linked up with some old friends and hung out around the city, and had a blast enjoying my old environment. Then, the Fourth of July arrived, and I realized I had an issue I hadn't been aware of.

Each time fireworks exploded it felt like my

heart was going to burst its way out of my chest. I was having panic attacks. I did all that I could to not allow the people around me to realize how much I was suffering. They wouldn't understand my feelings. They couldn't. They hadn't been through what I had experienced in the war.

Two weeks passed, and the time came to head back to Iraq. I hugged my mom and dad and then boarded the first of my multiple flights back to Iraq. When I arrived back at Camp Anaconda, I exited a plane and hopped into the back of a truck that would take me and others back to the area we lived on in the camp. Once we arrived, I jumped off the truck went inside the building, sat down, and within a couple of minutes, there was an explosion. The whole building rocked violently.

One of my buddies looked at me with complete shock and said, "Someone must be praying for you." We went outside and discovered the row of vehicles in front of the building had been heavily damaged. There was damage to parts of the building as well. The truth of what my friend had said to me hit me hard. Had I arrived a couple of minutes later than I did, I would have been hit by the mortar that had landed and likely would have died.

I continued attending those choir rehearsals and Sunday services. They were extremely comforting. During the Sunday services, they would ask you to stand if it was your last week in the war and you would be heading home before the next service. For an entire year, I watched people stand each week, and eventually my turn to stand came. It was time to go home. There was an issue getting a charter flight to take us back to

Hawaii, so we were given the option of going home on a C-17 cargo plane. We accepted the offer. I flew from Iraq to Hawaii on a C-17, with its thick, netted seats.

I am forever grateful for those who greeted us when we made the first stop on American soil. One of them gave me a calling card, and I ran to a pay phone and called my parents to let them know that I had made it back to the United States. We eventually made it to Hawaii after a few more stops. There were many family members and friends waiting to greet us as we returned. I watched the tearful reunions between husbands and wives. I observed children greeting their military parent for the first time in a very long while. I looked on as friends greeted one another with extreme joy. All of this was bittersweet. I had no one to greet me. I boarded a bus and went back to an empty barracks room. All my belongings, including my vehicle, were in storage. I sat in my empty room, alone and with nothing, and tried to find some form of meaning in the silence.

(13)

Survival

I WANTED TO stay in the Army. I attempted to reenlist as a chaplain assistant, but I ran into obstacles and decided to give up on that and move on to civilian life. I had a totally unrealistic expectation of what life would be like outside of the military. I had this grand plan of all that I would do and accomplish, but I was about to be hit with some hard forms of reality.

The day I landed in Little Rock Arkansas, my mother picked me up from the airport and I asked her to take me to a recruiting station for the Air National Guard, immediately after leaving the airport. I joined the Air Guard that same day and I chose the job of services technician. I would be required to attend one weekend drill per month and participate in two weeks of training each summer. I first had to go to San Antonio, Texas, for a month and a half for training to learn how to perform my job.

Having made it back to El Dorado, Arkansas, I was living in the same home I grew up in with my parents, and I can't imagine what my parents must've been feeling back then. They had seen me leave and go out into the world to become a man, and now I was back at home, right where I'd started. I tried hard to find a job, but there were no jobs available. I began to see how difficult life was going to be for me in my old hometown. I had thought that my military experience would guarantee me a job, but that was far from being true. My only break from reality was my girlfriend at the time. I spent a lot of time with her and that kept me from having to think about my circumstances, but she had a job and I didn't. That was a hard pill for me to swallow.

During the summer of 2005, I had to go with my Air Guard unit to Gulfport, Mississippi, for annual summer training. It was surreal to be there. I had attended engineering training in Gulfport while in the Army, and now I was back, but in totally different circumstances. Once we returned home from Gulfport, I got into my car and began to head back home to El Dorado. While driving, I came to the dismal realization that my life was going nowhere. I knew I couldn't go back to El Dorado. I turned the car around and drove to Conway, Arkansas, just north of Little Rock, and went straight to the home of my aunt and uncle. I told them I needed a place to stay until I could find a job. My uncle gave his approval and told me I could stay as long as I wanted. I had no intention of staying very long though. I was such an independent person, and I always have been. I was determined to find a job and a place of my own as soon as possible. Looking back on the time, I probably should have stayed longer than I did.

I found a job loading luggage onto airplanes at what is now known as the Bill and Hillary Clinton National Airport in Little Rock. The job paid $7.45 per hour, and the length of the shifts changed from week to week. I needed 40 hours per week, but there was no guarantee that I would get that many hours. Even so, I was able to get an apartment. My uncle told me I could continue staying until I got on my feet, but I was determined to be independent, and I didn't want to drive from Conway to Little Rock and then back to Conway every day.

My uncle helped me pick up my things from my parents' home in El Dorado. The furniture and other items I had in Hawaii had been shipped there, and it was time to take them to my new home. My new apartment felt more like a cave than a home. It sat at the base of a hill in a somewhat urban neighborhood. The apartment building was three stories, but due to the hill in front of it, you would walk onto the third floor at ground level and then have to work your way down to the lower levels. I lived on the second floor. I don't know why the builder bothered to place a window in the apartment, because there was a concrete wall against the hill a few feet outside my window, so I had no view. I earned enough money to pay rent, make my car payment, pay utility bills and almost nothing else.

One day I'm sitting in my apartment starving, and my neighbor across from me begins to barbecue on his grill. The smell is coming beneath my door and hitting me right in the face. I'm starving and having to smell the aroma of food at the same time. I had no choice but to go out and see if by some miracle he would offer me something to eat. I exited my apartment and said, "Hello." A conversation started and eventually he invited me to share a meal with him. From then on, he and I would have some great conversations daily. He was the only person I associated with in the building. The apartment had a lot of negative activity around it. I remember one day I was leaving, and I heard one of my neighbors screaming. As I walked past the half-open door of his apartment, He screamed,

"Help me."

I knew of him, vaguely. He had a drug habit and had been causing a lot of unwanted circumstances around the building. As I walked past the door, those inside looked at me and I looked at them. But I kept walking. I didn't call the police or try to help. I didn't know what to do. All I knew was that I had better go to work, because if I missed even one minute that could be the difference between being able to pay rent and eat or being homeless and starving. I saw him the next day. You could tell he had been beaten. It bothered me that I hadn't tried to help him. The beatings he took, however, didn't seem to shake him. His drug habit persisted, and his dealings/friendship with those same individuals who had beaten him continued.

On another occasion, I stepped out of my front door and was promptly greeted by a man with a sawed-off shotgun. I could tell by his face that he was there to use it. He looked at me, and I looked at him, and in an unspoken way we acknowledged each other, and I walked past him, barely an inch away. I knew he could possibly shoot me. I had seen his face. I didn't have time to consider it, because like I stated previously, I had to go to work or starve and be homeless. I made it to my car, and I left. When I returned home, all was well. I assumed whoever or whatever he had been hoping to find wasn't found that day.

I rarely had anyone come to my place. The distance had led to an end of my relationship with my girlfriend. On a few rare occasions, a girl would come to visit me, and my parents also came to visit a few times as well. I spent most of my time alone. At that point in my life, I was ignoring God. I rarely went to church. I never read my Bible and I never prayed. Life was about nothing more than just surviving.

(14)

PTSD & Comedy

AROUND THIS TIME, ironically, I discovered that I had a talent for comedy. My ability to make people laugh had been a tool used to keep others uplifted when I was in the military. It had also been a tool I used to keep myself encouraged when times got hard. After being encouraged to do so, I performed at an open mic event at a local comedy club, and the place went crazy. It was a great moment for me, standing in front of all the people and witnessing the joy I was bringing them. I realized I was great at this, so I made the decision to pursue comedy with an absolute passion. I started to get opportunities to perform around the city first, and then around the state, and then opportunities outside of the state began to come as well. I Just knew that this was what I was going to do with my life.

Through my performances, I started to make many friends. Life began looking up, and I even managed to find a better job. My uncle worked for a company that manufactured and sold private jets, and he informed me that the security department was hiring. This job paid much more than my old one, and the schedule allowed me to continue to do comedy shows and travel on weekends. Eventually, I was promoted to shift supervisor.

Life was not perfect by any means, but it was

good. I also started attending a local technical college, and later transferred to a university. I was so passionate about comedy that, when I was offered a greater employment opportunity, I turned it down because the schedule conflicted with my comedy opportunities. This was one of the many stupid things I would do for the sake of comedy. It had become the ultimate priority in my life above everything else. I started meeting celebrities, and people would come up to me after shows just to tell me how awesome I was after performing. I was totally caught up in pride and loving it.

One night, I was asleep and suddenly woke up with the most horrible feeling I had ever felt. I jumped out of bed immediately and could tell that something was very wrong. I ended up half-dressed and stumbling through the streets, trying to maintain my sanity and calm my rapid breathing. From that moment on, I experienced a tremendous struggle with PTSD, (Post-Traumatic Stress Disorder) in relation to my experiences during the war. There would be moments when the same feelings I had during the war would suddenly return and it was as if I were there again. I couldn't watch any movies that had any form of war in them, because it would trigger the PTSD and I would suddenly be fighting to keep my sanity. I hid it as best as I could.

I continued to perform comedy and put on a fake smile when I was around others, but there were times I couldn't fake it anymore. A couple of times I attempted to tell someone, but they didn't understand what I was trying to communicate with them. It started feeling pointless. On one occasion, I was at a weekend drill for the Air National Guard when I started to have an episode. My sanity was slipping away from me and no one around me knew it. I was in trouble and I knew it. If I didn't get some help soon, I wasn't going to make it.

Despite this struggle, things continued to improve in other parts of my life. I moved into a nice apartment in a great area with little crime. I even had multiple windows and none of them faced a concrete wall. Things continued to improve for me, and eventually, I was able to purchase a home. Although I had more material things in my life than many others, I was miserable and hurting tremendously inside. Eventually, by some stroke of divine intervention, I was told about a center that offered counseling services to veterans. I began going to appointments to see a counselor, and she was a significant help to me. I could tell her everything, and she knew how to respond in just the right way. I also began to go to church again.

The church I went to, had an amazing pastor. He always had a way to cheer me up, no matter how I was feeling. There were also an excellent group of men there, and once per week the men would all come together and sit in a circle and just talk. I could present an issue that was plaguing me, and they would listen and give advice from a Biblical perspective. There was a discipleship process in place at the church, which really helped me, but I wasn't as open as I should have been and neglected to allow the men around me to give me wisdom in relation to comedy. I believe God has given certain individuals the gift to make others laugh, but it must be submitted to His will for it. I failed to recognize this. I continued to do standup comedy. I was a "clean comedian," meaning that I refrained from cursing and my material could be performed anywhere, including family events. There were a few moments where I ventured into unclean material, but for the most part, I kept it family-friendly. By being a clean comedian, I could have access to more events, because I could perform at a birthday party or a club or even events where Christians were present. This love for comedy was so great that it caused me to leave the home I purchased, my well-paying job, and my new-found church family and friends.

I had flown to Los Angeles to audition for a movie, and while there I was completely blown away by the reception, I received from people I was used to seeing on television. I seemed to fit right in. I was given access that the average person would not have received, so I felt comedy must be my calling. When I returned to Arkansas, I felt that I needed to leave and head to a larger entertainment market. My initial urge was to move straight to LA. I had become friends with a popular entertainer, and he advised that I not move to Los Angeles until I had absolutely perfected my talent. He told me, "LA gives you one chance to show what you got, and if you blow it, you will likely never get another shot." With that in mind, I decided on Atlanta instead. So just like that, I up-rooted myself and moved to Atlanta, Georgia.

(15)

Atlanta

I WAS WARNED about the environment I was about to enter in Atlanta a couple weeks before moving. I had submitted a request to transfer with my company. I was off to bigger and better things, and I made sure everyone knew it. So, out of pride, I ignored the warnings. I packed a few things in my truck and drove eight hours to my new home in Atlanta without looking back. When I arrived, I received notice that my employee transfer never went through, because my previous location had not sent my HR files. Without those documents, I was left unemployed. As hard as I tried to get the matter settled, the files never came. With the country in a recession and most businesses unable to hire, I was left with no other option than to spend my time looking for a new job, networking and getting acquainted with my new environment. The lines at the centers that helped with finding employment were very long. A lot of people had moved to Atlanta due to the city's popularity and many had not secured employment before coming.

Every week, I attended church, and every week I met new and interesting people. The first unique experience came when I met a famous entertainer at church. I hadn't seen him in anything for a couple of years. He was sporadically dabbling in entertainment but seemed to be leaning more towards focusing on his walk with the Lord. The man knew his Bible. Scriptures would roll off his tongue and he would break down the interpretation of them for everyone to grasp. He also broke down the ins and outs of the world of entertainment including the good and the bad aspects of it. I also met an actor who helped me network even further, connecting me to people he knew and giving me access to the environments they inhabited. Atlanta was filled with entertainers and opportunities.

Little opportunities began to come. I performed comedy any and everywhere that I could. I'd go wherever, whenever. I remember discovering an upcoming show in the city. I wanted in. I called the promoter and sold myself, and when she agreed to let me be in the show, I was beyond hyped to have booked the opportunity. The problem however was that the acts were solely hip-hop performances, so I thought when people see me, they are going to be confused or angry. This was going to be hard. As the song being performed by the act before me faded out, the MC took the stage to announce my act. "We have a comedian in the house," she shouted. I watched the faces of the audience turn to stone. They weren't expecting that. I came forward, grabbed the microphone and went into my routine. Joke by joke, their faces softened, and their frowns turned to laughter. The place filled with hard laughter, and when I finished, they applauded me. I had succeeded. I pulled off the impossible, and it boosted my confidence. That was the moment I knew for sure that I could do comedy. I began meeting a lot of people that had come to Atlanta to become actors, actresses, singers, musicians, comedians and all sorts of talent. I seemed to get opportunities that many were not getting. I was always noticed, always offered opportunities, and I wasn't putting in half of the effort they did to get opportunities. I performed at private parties and received a small indie film opportunity. I was eventually able to link up with an entertainment executive and while with him I met the owner of a company that leased private jets. The owner of the jet company and I were speaking over the phone one day and he started offering flight options and deals on leasing time on the jets. If he knew what was in my bank account at the time and my financial status, he would have laughed at himself for trying.

More doors opened, as I eventually found a job with a regional security firm that offered a totally flexible schedule. Despite this, work and entertainment ventures still became conflicted. It was hard to find a balance. While performing at a private party one night, I was noticed by a guy who was a close friend of two world famous entertainers. He took me to meet them and I was speechless. Although it was a meet and greet type of opportunity, I felt like I had officially arrived. I received a few more opportunities to hang out with one of them. Eventually I was offered an opportunity to be on the set of some upcoming filming with the entertainer, by one of his closest friends and I was thrilled. If this went well, future opportunities would automatically come my way. But when I accepted the opportunity, work was the last thing on my mind. I forgot that I had promised my manager that I would work a shift plus overtime on the date of the filming. I contemplated what I should do. Should I call out sick? But if I did that, I may never get any more shifts and I needed the job. After wrestling with this for a while. I decided I had to go to work and miss the filming. Work was paying and hanging around a set during filming was not. Rent for my apartment would be due soon and I had better go get the money.

I grew lonely. I had no family, and my real friends in Atlanta were from the city and spent time with their families. I decided it was time to find someone to settle down with. I wanted someone who would support my dreams and goals but attempts at fulfilling this were unsuccessful. Something always seemed to go wrong when I thought that I had found the lady I was looking for.

An example would be a time in which I brought a real close friend of mine along with me to meet a girl I'd been pursuing because her friend would be with her also. After my friend had a couple of drinks and he started having a heart-to-heart conversation with everyone. I learned more about him in then, than I ever had previously. He talked about a time when he was locked up in a psych ward after losing his mind. That was just one of his disclosures. On the way back to our section of the city, I'm like, "yo, you was locked up in a psych ward?" He replied, "yeah man." After that night, the girl became distant and never gave me much time, so I was forced to move on. Maybe my friend's story was a bit much for her. I wasn't willing to drop him as a friend. He had come through for me big time on several occasions when I was in need and if he was your friend, you had a solid dude with you.

I started to fill a real void within me. No matter what I did, and the amount of fun doing it, and no matter what I gained, I still had to return home to the empty four walls of my apartment feeling lonely, unsatisfied and empty. Eventually, I broke. I gave in. I realized there was nothing to enjoy outside of Jesus Christ. I found a great church and started to attend Sunday services regularly. The sermons convicted me and helped me grow. I started going to the weekly Bible studies. The pastor was very encouraging to me. He motivated me to draw closer to God. I remember he preached a sermon titled, "What's Driving You." That question hit me right in my soul and forced me to take inventory of my life. I started to change. Entertainment was no longer a priority. I stopped pursuing all opportunities.

Around this time a special friendship began to develop into something more. I met a girl for the first time when I was a kid and the first time that I saw her, I was speechless. My father had come home one day and told us we were going to visit a church that he felt led to attend and I really didn't want to go. When I arrived and saw this girl, my attitude changed completely. I didn't understand it at the time, but somehow as a child, I knew that there was something significant about this girl regarding myself. Her name was Charlissa and she had moved to Arkansas when she was 11 with her grandmother. We grew up together as nothing more than friends and when she reached adulthood, she went her way and when I reached adulthood, I went mine.

Charlissa eventually moved back to California, where she was originally from. I had learned that she was divorced and had two kids. We had regained contact with each other two years before I had moved to Atlanta and I had flown to California to visit her twice from Arkansas, but we settled on the fact that we would never be more than just friends.

I started flying to see her again from Atlanta to Bakersfield, California. Eventually, we began to officially date. This was both great and challenging due to the 2,193 miles between us. I loved making the trips. The kids were awesome, and I always looked forward to seeing them. Francesca was the oldest, a beautiful little girl with a bright smile. She wrote a letter to her mother telling her she should marry me. I still have it today. The little man, Evan, always had a smile on his face and was a joy to be around also.

One day, I considered the fact that I had always flown to Bakersfield, so I decided to fly Charlissa to Atlanta for the first time. We had an incredible time while she was there. The day before she was going to leave, I realized I couldn't do the long-distance relationship anymore. I knew that the next time I saw her I wanted us to be together forever and no more flying back and forth. With no prior preparations or intentions. I suddenly asked her to marry me. She asked me if I was sure and I said, "yes, I'm sure." She said she had to think about it and the next day flew back to California. A day or so after that she called and said, "yes" to my proposal.

I thought she would move to Atlanta, but God revealed to me that He wanted me in California. In a subtle way, I had received this instruction before moving to Atlanta but ignored it, and now, I was being confronted with it again. After wrestling with this for a while, I chose to be obedient. On a rainy October day in Atlanta, I loaded my truck, and headed to Bakersfield, California.

(16)

God is Real

ONE THING STANDS out, as I consider those in scripture that chose to be obedient to God's will for their lives. They all suffered to some degree while fulfilling the Father's will. God had led me to leave Atlanta and head to California, and I was excited about that. I totally ignored the fact that there would be suffering associated with my obedience. Charlissa and I planned to marry in June of 2010, and not live together until we were married. I stayed in an extended-stay hotel until I could find an apartment.

In Atlanta, I lived in a really nice apartment. The area was safe, and I enjoyed frequent jogs through the neighborhood, around a small pond nearby. I didn't realize how good I had it in Atlanta until I reached California. However, with a pretty good amount of money in my savings and a new job opportunity lined up, I was confident in my move. I was tested when I moved to California. I had to prove that I trusted God and that I would be obedient, even in hardship. I didn't have a California driver's license, so the job I had lined up wouldn't allow me to go through the hiring process. I informed my potential employer that I would go to the DMV to get one right away, but it didn't work out. I'm not sure of why the license was such a big deal, because the job did not require me to drive.

With no job on the horizon, I was forced to only

shop for the cheapest food and other necessities, but nothing was cheap. Everything was far more expensive than Atlanta. Registering my vehicle was unreal. The cost was astronomical in comparison to anywhere else I had ever lived. I had to retake a written driving exam as if I never had a license and then pay a fee to get the license. Little expenses like this started to chip away at my savings. I completed so many job applications and didn't receive any opportunities. It was a very depressing time. One day I get back to my hotel room after being unsuccessful at finding any work and I began eating a really cheap rotisserie chicken I purchased at a grocery store and I immediately realized why the chicken was so cheap. It was as dry as desert sand. I had to chew each piece hundreds of times before attempting to swallow any of it. That day was an all-time low for me. I would have cried if my pride hadn't gotten in the way.

Talking with others in the hotel helped me through the process. We were each stuck due to a variety of circumstances. It was nice to speak with individuals that were facing similar hardships. We could relate with one another in an effortless way. There was an older gentleman living next door to me who seemed to love living in the hotel. He had no intentions of leaving. I, however, was more than ready to leave. The struggle to secure a job was taking its toll on me. I was broken and feeling as though things would never get better. Nothing seemed to be working out, and some days, I struggled to maintain any joy at all.

One day I discovered a courier job opening, so I went to the company business office to apply. While completing the application, an employee was struggling with an item he was trying to get into a truck, and he asked for my assistance. After I helped him, he told the manager to hire me, highlighting my eagerness to help. The manager gave me a verbal confirmation that the job was mine, but as we said our goodbyes, another man walked in to apply. He and the manager knew each other, and I watched them greet one another as though they were extremely happy to see each other. The man told the manager he was down on his luck and in need of a job desperately. I left hoping the job was still mine, but I couldn't keep doubt from creeping in. I never got a call from the manager, and I'm sure the guy who came in after me received it. That was the closest I had come to getting a job thus far and nothing else came anywhere close to that opportunity.

One day, I was so sad and stressed about not being able to find work that I wasn't thinking properly while driving. I made a sharp move to change lanes and totally failed to see that there was a car alongside me. I smashed right into the vehicle of an elderly lady. I was shocked that she never pulled over so that we could exchange insurance information. After following her for a while I decided to stop, because she seemed very scared and I didn't want her to think that I was trying to harm her. I headed back to the hotel for the rest of the day.

My pastor at the time was a tremendous blessing. I stuck as close to him as I possibly could. I had never seen anyone with a heart for God as great as his heart was toward the Lord. During times of prayer, he would pray for things that were affecting me without even knowing it. My greatest appreciation was the accountability I had under him. He was like a father figure to me. In times of correction, he reprimanded me, and in moments of hopelessness, he offered encouragement. God used him to teach me many things about the faith. For the first time, I was fully engaged in discipleship under a leader, with no distractions. He even provided me with little opportunities to earn money doing odd jobs around the church. Each time I gathered with my church or worked on anything they needed, I received the strength to keep going despite the obstacles I faced.

Though my faith grew stronger as time went on, my finances were still weak. Eventually I was forced to tell Charlissa that I would have to return to Atlanta to regroup and maybe give California a try again in the future. I had gone as far as I could go, and from my perspective, I had reached a dead end. A few days later, I saw the sign of a familiar security company I had worked for part-time years before in Arkansas to make a little extra money. I was surprised to see that they had an office in Bakersfield. I went back to the hotel immediately and completed an online application and a miracle happened! The next day, the company called. They wanted an interview with me immediately. I went in for the interview and they offered me a part-time position as a security officer at a local healthcare company. Now, with a secure job, although part-time, Charlissa and I decided to get married within the next couple of weeks instead of waiting until June of 2010. On December 19, 2009, I married my best friend. Though I thanked God for my job and for bringing me through tough circumstances, I still needed more money to support my new family. I prayed for help, and guess what? Another miracle happened. I discovered that the

Army was paying individuals who were held past their contract during the war. I completed the required paperwork and had almost forgotten about it. I went to the ATM one day to get what little money I had in it and there was $5,500 in my account. My heart was overwhelmed with joy that day. I was able to pay off some debts and still had plenty of money remaining. Financial miracles like this, although not as large, started to occur frequently during the early years of our marriage. Needs would arise, and miracles would occur.

It took me a while to get adjusted to being married and I made a lot of mistakes in the beginning. I was so used to being single that I failed to realize marriage demanded a constant sacrifice. I couldn't play basketball every day or make decisions based on what I wanted, because my decisions didn't just affect me, they affected my family as well. I also failed to realize that it would take time for the kids to get adjusted to me being around all the time. To win them over, it would take time and consistency from me to prove that I loved and cared for them. I tried to win them over quickly by giving them money and gifts, but it would only work temporarily. I had to learn to be patient.

The summer of 2010 brought a small revival to my church that lasted a few nights. I was feeling very gloomy at the time and wasn't up to going so I happily went to work on the first night of the gathering. However, I did make it to the second night of the gathering. I was in awe of what I saw. The Holy Spirit was moving in a mighty way in that place. The minister who spoke that night began displaying powerful gifts. People were being healed, delivered from demonic strongholds and given prophetic messages. At one point during the service, he turned and looked straight at me. "You," the minister shouted in my direction. He began to tell me things only known by God and myself. He spoke about my regret of moving, my complaints about my income, and my struggle with being who I needed to be in my marriage. I was blown away by his knowledge of intricate details of my life and his knowledge of things I had only thought and had never told anyone. As he spoke, my hands rose as though I were surrendering. When he finished speaking to me the Holy Spirit fell on me and filled every fiber of my being. Everything around me faded, and the only voice I heard was my own. All I could see was a flame-like mist swirling in patterns. All I could think was, "Wow! God is real!"

That moment was the most wonderful experience I have ever had. When it was finally over, I felt brand new. From that day forward, I was 100% committed to walking with God. I was equipped to be the man I needed to be for my family. I had the ability to be faithful to my church, and I was ready to do whatever God wanted me to do.

There were gifts imparted into me that night that I did not have before. I started to read the Bible as God's word and not like a regular book. The scriptures came alive within me as I read them. When I would share my faith, I saw the impact it had on others, which was much different than before. Individuals were moved by my words when I spoke. I woke up daily committed to looking for opportunities to share my faith. I now had the ability to say no to sin that I was a slave to before. My mind was sharper than it had ever been. I could truly love people the way believers are called to love, sacrificially. That began my journey to truly pursue God's purpose for my life. I was faithful in my local church and was eventually made a deacon. A couple of years later, I became a minister.

Within months, I officially became an elder within the church. I continued to learn many things from my pastor and the other elders of the church. The men that surrounded me during my time there will never know the magnitude of how much God used them to shape me into a better man and a dedicated follower of Jesus. This was a wonderful period in my life that I will always remember. It was in this time that I matured spiritually in a significant way.

(17)

Another Transition

MY PART-TIME security position eventually led to greater employment opportunities that allowed me to adequately provide for my family. I became very comfortable in life, but once again, God instructed me to move. I wrestled with this for quite some time, second-guessed it, and even fought it. I really loved my pastor and my church. I couldn't fathom leaving them behind and starting over in a new place. But I ultimately decided to be obedient and began applying for jobs within my company in different cities throughout Southern California and in Atlanta. I received a phone interview for a job in Atlanta and it seemed that I would be heading back to my former city. At the end of the process another individual was chosen over me because he or she already lived in Atlanta. So, I continued to apply for positions within the company nation-wide.

One Friday morning, I didn't have to work, and I felt a strong urge to take a ride in my car. I told my wife that I felt the Lord was urging me to take a drive and that I would be heading out for a while. Prior to this a friend who attended my church told me that it was revealed to him that I would be moving south. I drove as I felt led heading south and eventually made it to a city called Woodland Hills in the San Fernando Valley area of Los Angeles. I took a restroom break at a hospital and then continued to drive west.

Driving down the 101 freeway I came to an area near the town of Newbury Park, where the freeway begins a steep decline into a valley like area. From this point you can see a small glimpse of the Pacific Ocean in the far distance ahead, on a cloudless day. Just as I came upon the peak, but before the decent I had an incredible experience. It was as though a window was opened and a fresh wind of clean air hit me. Tears began to flow, and I began to give God Praise. I knew I had found the place that I had been called to. I continued to drive as I felt led and eventually made it to the beachside community of Port Hueneme, CA. At that moment, I remembered listening to a minister on the radio a year or more prior. He asked God if he should live in a particular city, and as he prayed on it, he sat on a wall within the city. As I drove through this area, I suddenly came to a section of beach, which had a just below waist high wall that stretched for a considerable distance. Without hesitation, I parked and sat on the wall and prayed. I told the Lord that if He wanted me in that area, I was willing to be there.

A couple of weeks after this experience, I received a call from the same hospital I had stopped at during the drive to use the restroom, and I was offered an interview for a job. I had applied for a job there a month or two prior. I went to the interview, and it went well. I eventually received the job. I then prayed and asked the Lord to provide a church for my family to attend before we moved. He answered that prayer. I once had a website in which I wrote faith-based articles and conducted interviews. It was called, "The Only Door." It was a reference to Jesus Christ based on John 10:9-16. I reached out to a pastor on the East Coast to set up an interview and while talking with him, I mentioned that I was preparing to move to Los Angeles. He referred me to a church located in the Crenshaw area of Los Angeles. Several confirmations occurred to show me that it was the church I was to serve at.

With a job secured and a church to attend, I began to make the transition, but while making the transition, life became very difficult for my family. My kids had 6 more months of school, and we had to keep our place in Bakersfield for a couple of months until the lease expired. I also had to start at my new job. I attempted to rent out a room in several homes but was unsuccessful at doing so. One opportunity finally came through, but I quickly realized it was not a good place for me to be, so I made the hard decision to make the drive between Bakersfield and Woodland Hills during the 4 days per week that I worked.

The drive usually lasted one hour and forty-five minutes, but during morning and evening traffic it could significantly extend. Getting into Los Angeles in the morning was hard and leaving in the evening was even harder. During the drive I had to travel through a mountainous area called the "Grapevine." This can be a real challenge during the winter. One night, while attempting to make it back to Bakersfield, it began to snow tremendously. I could barely see more than a few feet in front of me. Somehow, I made it through the storm and came down from the mountains into the Central Valley and then on to Bakersfield.

The hardest challenge during this time occurred when I somehow developed an umbilical hernia, which required surgery. God blessed me with a great manager who was totally supportive during this time. I had to go on medical leave and have the required surgery to repair the hernia. The surgery went well, but I was left with chronic pain that plagues me to this day.

If that weren't enough trouble, a more significant issue arose. My wife and I had been legal guardians of our niece, for 7 years at this point. The Lord began revealing to me that we were to let her go. Of all the hard things I have had to do in my lifetime, this is undoubtedly the hardest. I really wrestled with this. I hesitated at first and the more I hesitated the harder the circumstances became to hold onto her. She had wanted to leave us, thinking it would lead to her being reunited with her mom. We tried unsuccessfully to explain that this would likely not happen. If I were in her situation at such an early age, I would probably think the way that she did also. Things eventually reached the point of impossible and I obeyed the Lord's instructions and let go. My wife and I received a massive amount of criticism for doing this. I feel tears in my eyes, just thinking about it. Letting my niece go was already hard enough, but now everyone around us had so many negative things to say about it. I had been obedient to God's instructions and was now suffering tremendously for it. I eventually decided the suffering was worth it to know that I had been obedient to God.

My wife and I also began to experience a consistent flow of occurrences that required money to resolve. These occurrences happened so frequently that eventually our savings account was completely drained. As hard as this was, each time an issue developed, a way was made for us to overcome it. I knew the Lord was watching over us. Through it all, I pressed forward.

I attempted so many times to find a place near the church or near my job, and nothing worked out as I had planned. I knew finding a place in Los Angeles would be difficult, but I hadn't realized how challenging it was until this experience. Eventually, with my back against the wall, I remembered the drive that I had taken to Port Hueneme, but a problem arose with this option. Port Hueneme is a 45-minute drive to Woodland Hills where I was working. It was also one hour and fifteen minutes from the church in Crenshaw. That wouldn't work at all. Running out of time, I finally decided to look for a place in Port Hueneme.

I found a place and was told I could come and check it out. I loved it, so I made a second trip there with my wife to get her thoughts. She loved it as well and we submitted an application. We were approved and received the keys. The rental agent told us that the property is usually filled within a day or two of becoming vacant but had been open for two weeks and not a single person inquired about it. The rent had been lowered prior to our application also due to the lack of interest in the place. I was now officially living in the place I was called to live, and I was ok with the commute to work, but church was far away. This was a hard decision, but ultimately, I chose to be part of the church anyway and make the sacrifice, after feeling led by the Lord to do so.

This is not unique to me. My father had experienced the same thing and was an assistant pastor for a church that was in a different town than the one we lived in for years. My grandfather had done the same as a pastor and I have uncles that have also served as pastors in towns and cities other than the ones in which they lived. It's as if long commutes to church are a calling for our family.

Some great friends opened their home in Bakersfield and allowed my wife and the kids to stay with them after the lease expired on our place there. My wife and the kids would travel to Port Hueneme on the weekends until the school year ended. Today we currently live in Port Hueneme and we travel into the city weekly, sometimes multiple trips per week, to support the church we attend in Crenshaw. I am now able to work two days per week close to home and two days in Woodland Hills. I continue to follow the leading of the Lord and I see Him doing incredible things at this point of my life. I take my walk with Him very serious and it is my will to do all that He calls me to do and be who He calls me to be.

At the moment, I can't say that I specifically know why God has called me to Port Hueneme, but I do know that I am called to be here. As time goes on, I see confirmations of this more frequently. Please pray that I would fulfill God's will for me in this place.

(18)

Conclusion

HOPEFULLY, THIS BOOK will make a few things evident.

1. **God loves us.** This is evident in the fact that He was with me even from the beginning, and although I faced difficult moments, His love for me never ceased. He loved me even when I rejected Him. He never gave up on me, and likewise, He will never give up on you.

2. **God's intervention is awesome.** There are many moments in which you can see God's intervention in my life. Those moments were very beneficial. Consider the moments of his intervention in your life.

3. **God's plan is the best plan.** The move from Atlanta to Bakersfield required faith. Within a few months of becoming a part-time security officer, I gained a full-time position, and a few months after that, I became the manager of my department. There were still difficult moments. The manager position was a 24/7 assignment that required a lot of sacrifices, but God saw me through it. Eventually, I received a tremendous opportunity to work for the client company. I could have stayed in Atlanta where I was comfortable, but God drew me to Bakersfield to mold me and shape me for His purpose. I've learned that when the Lord gives a

command, we must simply obey and trust Him. He has a plan — and that plan is perfect.

4. **My stumbling was a result of neglecting vital areas of the Christian faith.** After coming to faith in Jesus, I neglected three key areas of my walk as a Christian. I failed to engage in consistent prayer. I failed to consistently read the Bible. I also failed to allow myself to go through the discipleship process and build relationships with other Christians. It is often a challenge to balance these areas in the face of life's daily obligations, but we must make time for each of them.

5. **I am still not perfect.** I still make mistakes and fall short, but the Lord continues to mold me. I can say that I am no longer a slave to sin, nor am I the person that I use to be. I now wake up every day seeking to be used by God. I want to reach at least one individual with the glorious gospel of Jesus Christ daily. I have had many encounters with many individuals, and I have seen the Lord do marvelous things. As I look back, I see Jesus was with me the entire time. Before the earth was formed, the Father had chosen me, Ephesians 1:4, (NIV).

The Bible speaks of a Samaritan woman who had an encounter with Jesus at a well, and that encounter led her to go throughout her town to compel others, saying: "Come, see a man who told me everything I ever did. Could this be the Messiah," (John 4:29)? Just like the Samaritan woman, I am speaking to as many individuals as I can, and I'm telling them about Jesus. That's the purpose of this book, to share my testimony in an effort to point individuals to Jesus. Now, I tell you: Come and meet the Son of God, who took upon Himself the sins of the world so that we might experience true freedom and forgiveness.

"If you declare with your mouth, "Jesus is Lord," and believe in your heart that God raised him from the dead, you will be saved." Romans 10:9 (NIV)

Richard Smith

Thank you for taking the time to read this book. Please visit **Certaintyperspectives.com** and sign up for my email newsletter.

Certainty Perspectives

More books available at Certaintyperspectives.com

Therefore, if anyone is in Christ, the new creation has come: The old has gone, the new is here! 2 Corinthians 5:17 (NIV)

Acknowledgment

I would like to thank my wife Charlissa for her support and encouragement while I completed this literary work.